Contents

What is space?

When you are outside on a clear night, look up at the sky. You are staring into space. You can see hundreds of twinkling stars. Gazing at the stars at night is the best way to understand how vast and distant space is.

Scientists called **astronomers** also look into space. They use powerful telescopes to learn more about space and the **Universe**. We use the word Universe to mean everything that exists, from our **planet** Earth to the most distant parts of space.

Earth from space

We have been able to see the Earth from space for 50 years. Photos taken by **satellites** show us the Earth as a blue ball with green and brown land covered by swirling white clouds.

Where does space start?

We are surrounded by a layer of air called the atmosphere. Imagine the Earth is an orange. The atmosphere is like the peel wrapped around the orange. There is no exact place where the atmosphere ends and space begins, but it is about 100 kilometres above us, in the top part of the atmosphere.

Our planet Earth

The Earth is a planet in the **Solar System**. It is the only planet in our Solar System where there is life. There is oxygen in the Earth's atmosphere and there is water on the surface of the Earth. We need both oxygen and water to survive.

In fact the Earth should really be called Water, because the oceans and seas cover two-thirds of the surface. That is why the Earth looks mainly blue from space.

The inside of our planet is very different from the outside – inside it is so hot that rock melts.

How did the Earth begin?

Scientists think the Earth formed as a ball of hot liquid rock 4,600 million years ago. After millions more years it had cooled down enough for solid rock to form the **crust**. This is the outer part where we live.

Inside the Earth

Land and sea are
on the surface.

The centre is
very hot.

The inside is rocky.

The Earth's atmosphere
protects us from the
harmful rays of the Sun
and prevents the Earth
from becoming too hot
or too cold. We are just
the right distance away
from the Sun for life
to exist.

A satellite photograph showing the
Earth with deep blue oceans, white
clouds and green-brown land masses

Night and day

The Earth goes around the Sun along a pathway called an **orbit**. It takes one year – 365 days – to complete an orbit.

While the Earth moves along this path, it also spins round (like a spinning top) on an imaginary spike. The spike joins the north and south **poles** and is called the **axis**.

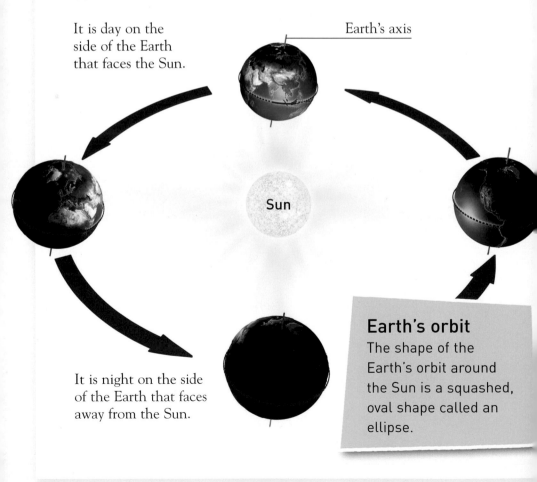

It is day on the side of the Earth that faces the Sun.

Earth's axis

Sun

It is night on the side of the Earth that faces away from the Sun.

Earth's orbit
The shape of the Earth's orbit around the Sun is a squashed, oval shape called an ellipse.

The Earth spins round on its axis once every 24 hours. The spinning gives us day (when one side faces the Sun) and night (when the same side faces away from the Sun).

At dawn it looks as if the Sun is rising above the horizon, but really it is the Earth that is moving.

The Moon

Our Moon moves around the Earth. Like Earth, the Moon is made of rock, but it has no air, no water and no life. It looks big because it is so close to us, but it is only a quarter the size of Earth.

There are thousands of craters on the surface of the Moon.

The Moon is covered with **craters** – saucer-like dents up to 1,000 kilometres across. They were made by **meteorites** that have crashed into it over billions of years.

The Moon also has human footprints and vehicle tyre tracks, made since humans first landed in 1969. It is the only place in the Solar System we have visited. The marks will be there for millions of years because there is no wind or weather to change the surface.

The Moon does not give out light of its own. The light we see is a **reflection** of some of the sunshine that falls on it.

The Moon orbits the
Earth while they travel
together around the Sun.

Phases of the Moon
As the Moon orbits the Earth, part or all of the side
facing Earth is lit by the Sun. It looks as though the
Moon changes shape from night to night. This
cycle takes 29.5 days, which is a lunar month.

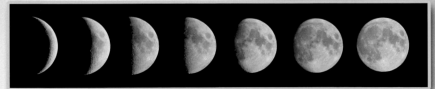

Mars – the red planet

If you see a reddish-orange object that looks like a star in the night sky, it is probably the planet Mars. It is called the red planet because the surface of dust and rocks looks orangey-red. Mars is named after Mars, the Roman god of war.

The biggest volcano in the Solar System is on Mars. It is called Olympus Mons.

Exploring Mars

Lots of unmanned **space probes** and space rovers have visited Mars and sent back pictures, but no human being has set foot on the planet – yet. At the moment, it would take about nine months to take a trip to Mars, and another nine months to come back again!

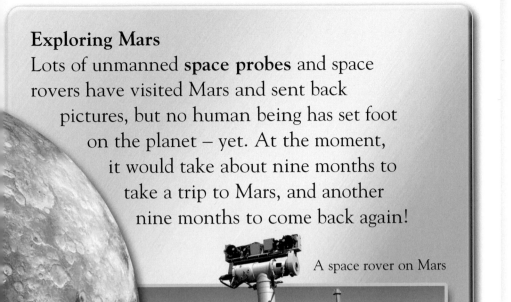

A space rover on Mars

Mars is a ball of rock with deserts, valleys, high mountains and volcanoes. It also has seasons, as Earth does. A year on Mars is nearly twice as long as an Earth year, but a day on Mars is about the same length as a day on Earth. The temperature on Mars is far, far colder than it is on Earth.

The giant planets

Four of the planets in our Solar System look like giant balls of gas from Earth. When we look at Jupiter, Saturn, Uranus and Neptune, we see the tops of their thick atmospheres. Deep inside, all the planets have a rocky **core**.

Jupiter is the biggest planet in our Solar System and it could swallow up more than 1,300 Earths. It spins around so fast that it creates coloured bands of clouds. One of these is a giant cloud called the

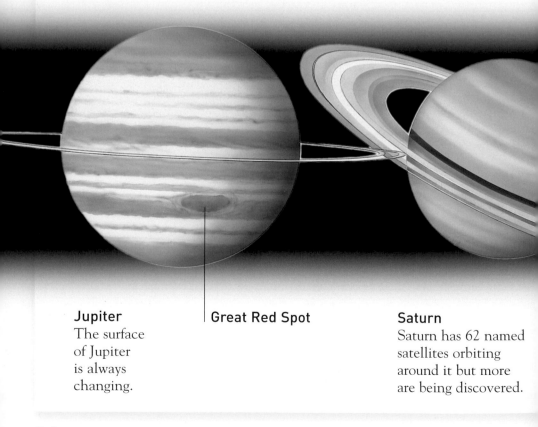

Jupiter
The surface of Jupiter is always changing.

Great Red Spot

Saturn
Saturn has 62 named satellites orbiting around it but more are being discovered.

Great Red Spot. This is a massive moving storm that has been raging for more than 300 years.

All the giant planets have rings around them, and Saturn's rings are the most extensive. Saturn's rings are made of countless pieces of ice, rock and dust.

Uranus and Neptune are similar, but Uranus is tilted on its side. Both these planets are about four times bigger than the Earth.

Uranus
Uranus was the first planet to be discovered after the telescope was invented.

Neptune
Neptune is the furthest planet from the Sun.

Here comes the Sun

For everyone who lives on planet Earth, the Sun is special. In fact the Sun is just an ordinary star – no bigger or shinier than others you see on a starry night. It looks bigger because it is closer than other stars – 150 million kilometres away. The Sun is our local star. This huge fireball gives us all our light and warmth and without it there would be no life.

How big?
You could fit 109 Earths side by side across the width of the Sun.

Huge clouds of gas flare up from the surface of the Sun.

The Sun
The temperature at
the surface of the Sun
is about 5,500°C.

Core

Surface

Close-up pictures show that the Sun
looks like a bubbling cauldron as
hot gases rush out. Some huge
flares of gas leap up so far
they completely escape. The
temperatures are so high that
at its core (centre) the Sun
makes **nuclear energy**, and
this makes it shine.

All living things depend on the Sun's energy.
Plants use it to grow and animals, including
people, depend on plants for energy.

The Solar System

The Earth is always moving around the Sun, along with other planets and smaller objects, including moons, **comets** and **asteroids**. The Sun and everything travelling around it make up the Solar System. The word 'solar' means to do with the Sun.

All these objects travel together along orbits around the Sun, because of the pull of the Sun's **gravity**. The further away a planet is from the Sun, the longer it takes to orbit (go round) it. Mercury is the nearest planet and it takes 88 days to orbit the Sun, Earth takes 365 days and Neptune takes more than 60,000 days!

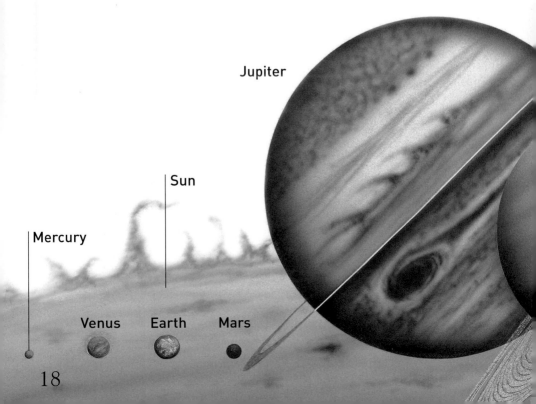

Jupiter

Sun

Mercury

Venus   Earth   Mars

The Solar System is vast. It is so big that it takes eight minutes for the Sun's light to reach the Earth. The spaces between the planets are huge compared with their size. Imagine you are holding a football. If the Sun was the size of the football, the Earth would be only half the size of a pea and nearly 25 metres away!

From biggest to smallest
The planets Jupiter, Saturn, Uranus and Neptune are much bigger than Earth, but Venus, Mars and Mercury are smaller.

Saturn

Uranus

Neptune

Our home galaxy

Our planet Earth is important to us, but it is just a little planet going around the Sun. The Sun is just one of a big group of stars called a **galaxy**. Our galaxy contains billions of stars and is called the Milky Way.

If you could travel out into space and look back, you would see that our galaxy is shaped like a flat disc with a bulge in the middle. Our Solar System is well away from the centre.

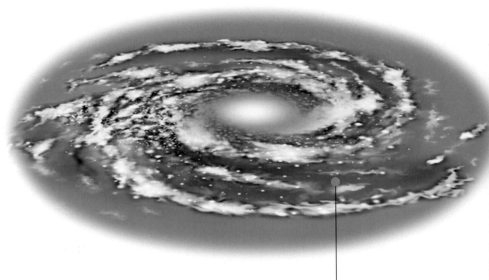

Our Solar System

Earth and our Solar System are a tiny part of the spiral galaxy called the Milky Way. All the stars we see at night are in the Milky Way.

Wherever you are on Earth, you should be able to see parts of the Milky Way in the night sky. Try looking for it on a very dark, clear night. If you have a telescope or binoculars, you will see masses of faint stars.

Galaxy shapes

Galaxies have different shapes. Some have **spiral** arms coming out of a circle. Some have spiral arms around a bar shape. Some are elliptical (egg-shaped) and a few are irregular (uneven) shapes.

Spiral galaxy

Barred spiral galaxy

Elliptical galaxy

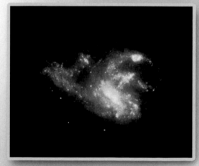
Irregular galaxy

The Universe

Universe is a word we use to describe everything that exists. This means everything we can see around us and also everything above us in the sky – our Moon, our Sun and our Solar System. Beyond that lies our galaxy, the Milky Way. Even further out are many more distant galaxies.

The Big Bang
Scientists know that our Universe is growing and cooling at the same time. They think that the Universe began as an explosion called the **Big Bang**. After the Big Bang, space was stretched out – imagine a balloon being blown up – over millions of years. At the same time the stars and planets were forming. The whole Universe is still expanding.

The Universe is made up of three basic things. There is ordinary **matter**, which makes the planets, stars and galaxies and other things we can see or measure. There is dark matter, a mysterious invisible mass found between the stars and galaxies. And there is dark energy, another invisible ingredient that scientists still don't understand.

This dark cloud of dust and gas is called the Horsehead Nebula. Can you see why?

This is the Andromeda Galaxy. It is the nearest large galaxy to the Milky Way.

The sky at night

Remember the nursery rhyme *Twinkle Twinkle Little Star?* The stars seem to twinkle when you look up at them on a dark, clear night. This is because we look up through air that is always moving about, so the starlight is unsteady and the stars seem to twinkle. If you could see a star from a spacecraft it would shine steadily.

These stars were painted in a tomb in ancient Egypt thousands of years ago.

From ancient times, people have looked at the stars and grouped them into shapes and patterns called **constellations**. The outlines were often based on old stories about people or animals such as a bull or crab. Ancient Greek, Arab and Chinese astronomers all gave names to the groups of stars they could see.

This picture shows astronomers looking at the sky hundreds of years ago in a place called Galatea, now part of modern-day Turkey.

The constellation Pegasus was named after a winged horse in ancient Greek mythology.

What is a star?

A star is an enormous spinning ball of hot, bright gases. The changing gases produce a lot of energy. Scientists call this nuclear energy and this is what makes stars shine.

A star starts as a ball of gas and dust which is pulled together strongly by gravity. The gas and dust get warmer and more squashed until the gas is so hot that nuclear energy is made. Then a star is born.

Stars are different colours because some are hotter than others. Cooler stars are more red and hotter stars look more bluey-white.

The life of a star

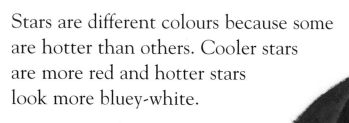

Stars begin life in a huge spinning cloud of gas and dust.

A part of the cloud comes together to make a star.

Billions of years later, towards the end of their lives, stars like our Sun become 100 times bigger.

Changing colours

When we heat a piece of metal the colours change. The metal glows red-hot, then it becomes brighter and more yellow until it is white hot. Stars shine in the same way depending on how hot they are.

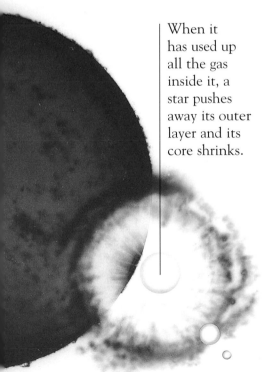

When it has used up all the gas inside it, a star pushes away its outer layer and its core shrinks.

Our Sun is a middle-aged star. Today it is classed as a yellow star. In about five billion years it will run out of gas and start to cool down.

Most stars then cool down and die.

Meteors

You can see many other objects in space on a clear night. You might see a point of light suddenly dart across the night sky. We call this a shooting star, but it is not a star at all – it is a meteor.

Barringer Crater in Arizona, USA

This piece of meteorite weighs 37g and was travelling at 72km per second when it hit the ground in Arizona.

Meteor showers

As the Earth travels round the Sun, it sometimes goes through a stream of space dust. When this happens we see meteor showers. These are spectacular groups of shooting stars.

Meteors streak across the sky.

A meteor is a streak of light made by a tiny piece of space rock or dust speeding through the Earth's atmosphere.

These tiny pieces of space rock burn up in the Earth's atmosphere, but some bigger ones get through and hit land or water really hard. These lumps of rock are meteorites. Some are big enough to make craters (like the craters on the Moon). The most famous crater on Earth is in Arizona in the USA. It was made more than 50,000 years ago and measures more than a kilometre across.

Comets

Comets are big lumps of snow and dust. There are millions of comets far out in space beyond the planets. Occasionally one travels towards the Sun and, as it gets close, it starts to melt and turn into gas. Bits of dust break off the comet and the gas and dust form a huge head and tails. A comet has two tails – one of gas and another of dust. The tails can be millions of kilometres long and they always point away from the Sun.

This comet, Hale-Bopp, was last visible in 1997. You can see its two tails.

Halley's Comet

Halley's Comet was named after Edmund Halley. He saw it in 1682 and was the first person to realize that it was a regular visitor. Chinese astronomers had seen it 2,000 years before that.

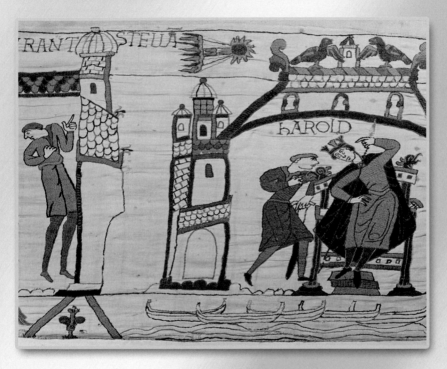

Halley's Comet was woven into the Bayeux Tapestry, which tells the story of the Battle of Hastings in 1066.

Some comets travel towards the Sun then move off into space and disappear. Others go round the Sun in long oval orbits. The most famous is Halley's Comet, which we can see from Earth every 75 to 76 years. The last time it passed was in 1986, and it is next expected in 2061.

Studying space

The study of objects in space is called astronomy.
Astronomers have studied the stars and estimated
sizes and distances in space since ancient times.
During the 1500s, an astronomer named Copernicus
showed that the Sun was in the centre of the Solar
System, with the planets orbiting around it.
Before then people believed that the Earth was
in the centre of the Universe.

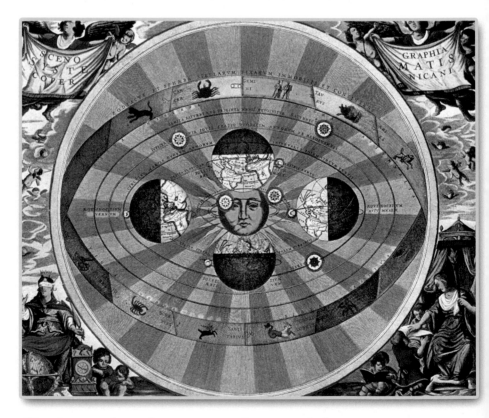

This diagram shows the astronomer Copernicus' idea
that the Sun is in the centre of the Solar System.

Studying space
Telescopes use lenses or mirrors to gather and focus the light from far away objects. This makes it easier to study outer space in detail.

In the early 1600s Galileo became the first person to use a telescope to look at the Sun, Moon and planets. His telescopes showed him the Moon's craters and mountains, as well as spots on the Sun's surface, four Moons around Jupiter, and many more stars. Galileo's telescopes made a huge difference to astronomy.

Radio telescopes have large metal dishes. Sometimes they are grouped together to gather more signals from space.

Space probes

Unmanned space craft sent out to explore our Solar System are usually called space probes. They carry powerful cameras and sensors to record what they see. There have been around 40 missions to Mars that have flown near or landed on the planet. Not all have been able to send back information; some probes have crashed or have lost contact with Earth.

Other space probes have orbited the Sun's poles, or flown past comets, or landed on an asteroid.

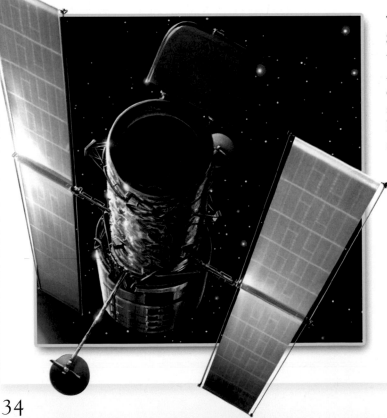

The Hubble Space Telescope was launched in April 1990 and orbits the Earth around 570 kilometres above us.

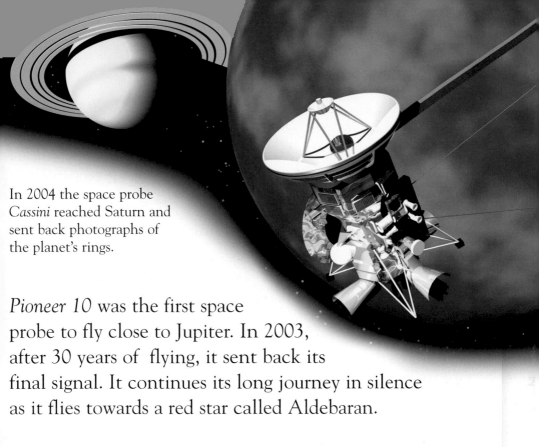

In 2004 the space probe *Cassini* reached Saturn and sent back photographs of the planet's rings.

Pioneer 10 was the first space probe to fly close to Jupiter. In 2003, after 30 years of flying, it sent back its final signal. It continues its long journey in silence as it flies towards a red star called Aldebaran.

Space telescopes study space from above our atmosphere and send back beautifully clear photos, as well as **X-ray**, **ultraviolet** and **infra-red** pictures.

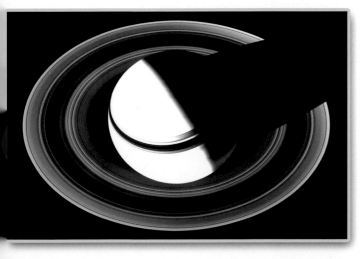

This photo of Saturn and its rings was taken by *Cassini*. The rings around Saturn are made of ice, rock and dust.

The race for space

The space age began in 1957, when Russia launched the first satellite, called *Sputnik 1*. It orbited the Earth for 98 minutes. It was the size of a beach ball and made of light metal with four **antennae**. A month later, *Sputnik 2* carried the first dog to orbit the Earth. Her name was Laika (meaning 'barker' in Russian).

In 1961 the Russian spacecraft *Vostok 1* carried Yuri Gagarin into orbit. He was the first man in space and spent 108 minutes there.

Laika inside a model of her space cabin

The Americans launched their space program with the Mercury space missions, and later the Gemini and Apollo missions. One month after Yuri Gagarin's trip, Alan Shepard became the first American in space.

Today people from many other countries, including China and Japan, have gone into space. Several countries worked together on the International **Space Station**, the biggest structure ever built in space.

Alan Shepard blasts off in 1961.

Space firsts

First satellite in space
Sputnik 1: 4 October 1957

First animal to orbit Earth
Laika on *Sputnik 2*:
3 November 1957

First man in space
Russian Yuri Gagarin
(*Vostok 1*): 12 April 1961

First woman in space
Russian Valentina Tereshkova
(*Vostok 6*): 16 June 1963

First walk in space

unattached to craft
American Bruce McCandless
(*Challenger*):
7 February 1984

Valentina Tereshkova

Man on the Moon

At 2.56 in the morning on 21 July 1969, astronaut Neil Armstrong said, "That's one small step for man, one giant leap for mankind." He had become the first human being to step on to the surface of the Moon.

Following Armstrong down the steps of the *Apollo 11* **lunar module** was fellow astronaut Buzz Aldrin. Together they took photographs, set up television cameras, planted a flag and collected Moon rocks.

More than 600 million people watched on television as the astronauts walked and hopped over the surface. On the Moon a person can jump six times as high as on the Earth because the Moon's gravity is weaker.

When the astronauts took off their helmets later, they described a strong smell like wet ashes in a fireplace. It was the Moon dust on their boots.

Every step the astronauts took threw up fine dust.

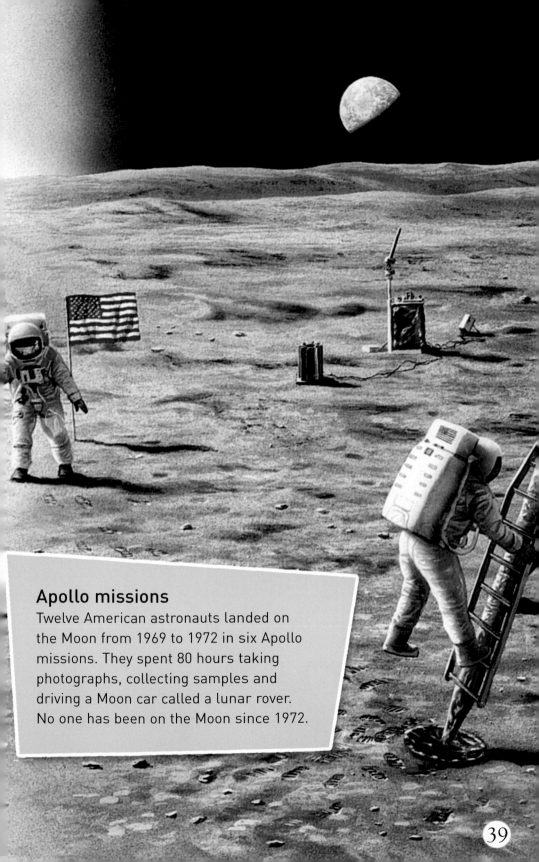

Apollo missions

Twelve American astronauts landed on the Moon from 1969 to 1972 in six Apollo missions. They spent 80 hours taking photographs, collecting samples and driving a Moon car called a lunar rover. No one has been on the Moon since 1972.

Space Shuttle

America's Space Shuttle was the first space plane. It was made up of three parts: the Orbiter, the booster rockets and the fuel tank. It flew into space more than 130 times.

The Orbiter was the size of a short-range airliner, with a flight cabin at the front and behind this an area for eating, sleeping and working. In another section it could carry space probes, telescopes, repair equipment and parts to build space stations.

The Space Shuttle lifted off from Earth like a rocket and the Orbiter returned like a glider plane.

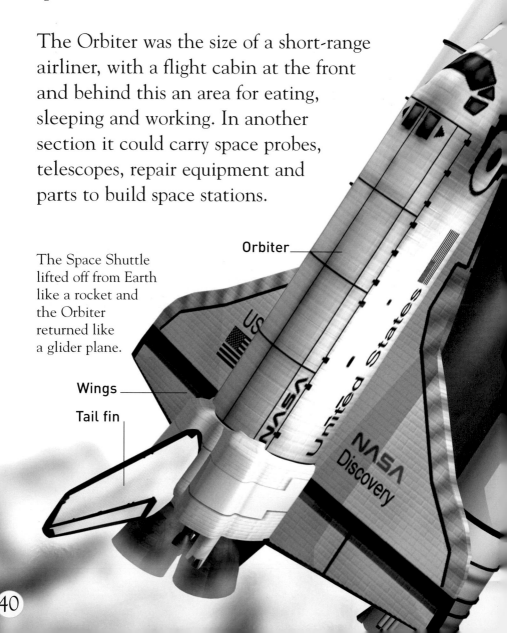

Orbiter

Wings

Tail fin

_____ Fuel tank

Two booster rockets helped to blast the Orbiter into space. They fell away into the sea and were found by ships. The only part not reused was the fuel tank, which was discarded once the fuel was used up. The Orbiter operated as a spacecraft in orbit around the Earth until it re-entered the atmosphere and landed on a runway, like a plane. A large parachute opened on landing to act as a brake.

_____ Booster rocket

The need for speed
To reach space we have to escape from the pull of gravity – the force which holds us down on Earth. The Space Shuttle reached a speed of more than 28,000km/h to get into orbit.

How to be an astronaut

Thousands of people apply to be an astronaut.
If you are chosen, you have to train very hard for
at least a year before you can go on a space flight.

All sorts of men and women become astronauts.
Many have studied science subjects at school
and afterwards at college.

All the parts of a
spacesuit lock together
so that the air inside
cannot escape.

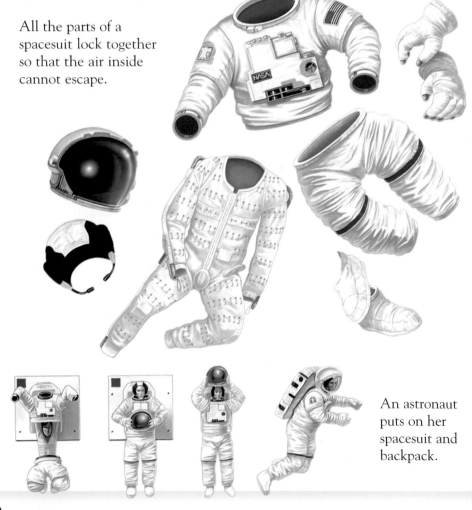

An astronaut
puts on her
spacesuit and
backpack.

Japanese astronauts float around in a
special aircraft, called the *Vomit Comet*,
to feel what it is like to be weightless.

Space agencies are looking for doctors, biologists,
geologists, engineers and people who have worked
in the armed forces, especially pilots.

Astronauts need to learn a lot about space flight and
spacecraft, and they need to be very fit. They train in
mock spaceships inside giant water tanks and take rides
in a diving aeroplane, to feel what it is like to be
weightless, like they will be in space. They learn to
work in bulky spacesuits and how to land with a
parachute on land or sea.

Space stations

A space station is a home in space. On board astronauts live, work and sleep as the station orbits around the Earth.

Astronauts don't wear spacesuits inside the space station. The cabins hold air to breathe and they protect the crew from harmful rays and dust. The biggest problem is weightlessness. Everything floats, including the astronauts, so they are strapped down to sleep and their food is strapped to their eating trays.

The ISS (International Space Station) is so large that we can see it at night from Earth. Different crews have lived on board for more than ten years. People can live on the ISS for many months at a time. Supplies and relief crews come aboard in a spacecraft that docks or links with the station.

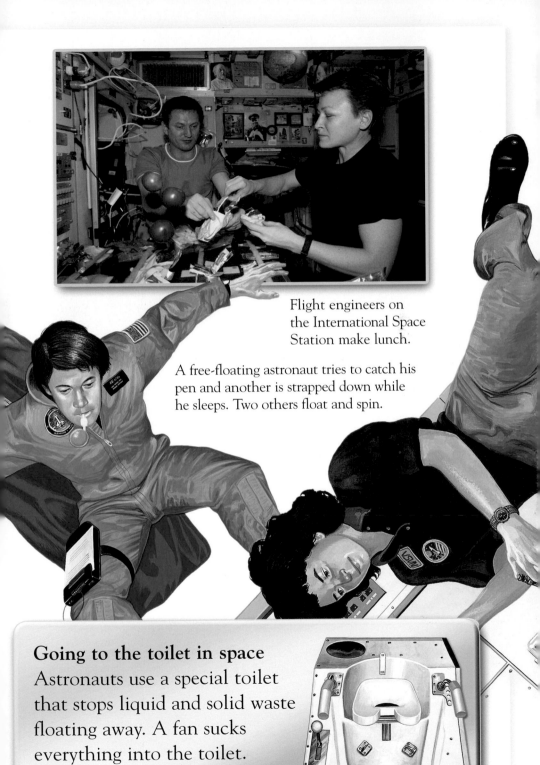

Flight engineers on the International Space Station make lunch.

A free-floating astronaut tries to catch his pen and another is strapped down while he sleeps. Two others float and spin.

Going to the toilet in space
Astronauts use a special toilet that stops liquid and solid waste floating away. A fan sucks everything into the toilet.

45

Glossary

antennae Devices that send out and receive radio, TV and satellite signals.

asteroid A small, rocky body that orbits the Sun.

astronomer Someone who studies the stars, planets and other bodies in space.

axis An imaginary line that an object spins round.

Big Bang The massive explosion that scientists think created the Universe.

comets Balls of frozen snow and dust that travel round the Sun.

constellations Patterns of bright stars that help us to spot and identify stars.

core The very hot centre of a planet or star.

crater A bowl-shaped hole made by a crashing meteorite.

crust The surface layer of a rocky planet or moon.

flares Exploding hot gases on the outer layer of the Sun.

galaxy A group of stars, dust and gas kept together by gravity.

gravity The force that pulls one thing towards another.

infra-red A type of light ray outside the range of visible light, which lets us see things using heat energy.

lunar module The landing craft which takes astronauts to the Moon's surface.

matter Anything that takes up space.

meteorite A piece of rock or metal from space which reaches the surface of a planet or moon without breaking up.

nuclear energy A source of power which is released when the structure of atoms is altered.

orbit The path of one object in space around another.

planet A large, round body made of rock or gas that orbits a star.

poles The two points (north and south) where the axis touches the Earth's surface.

reflection Light, heat or sound bouncing back from a surface.

satellite An object orbiting a planet. There are natural satellites, such as moons, and man-made ones, such as space telescopes.

Solar System The Sun and everything that orbits it.

space probe An unmanned spacecraft sent from Earth to explore the Solar System.

space station A spacecraft big enough for people to live and work on.

spiral A type of galaxy in the shape of a wheel.

ultraviolet A type of light ray outside the range of visible light.

Universe The whole of space and everything it contains.

X-ray A powerful wave of energy that helps us see through some objects.

Index